My Super Mother

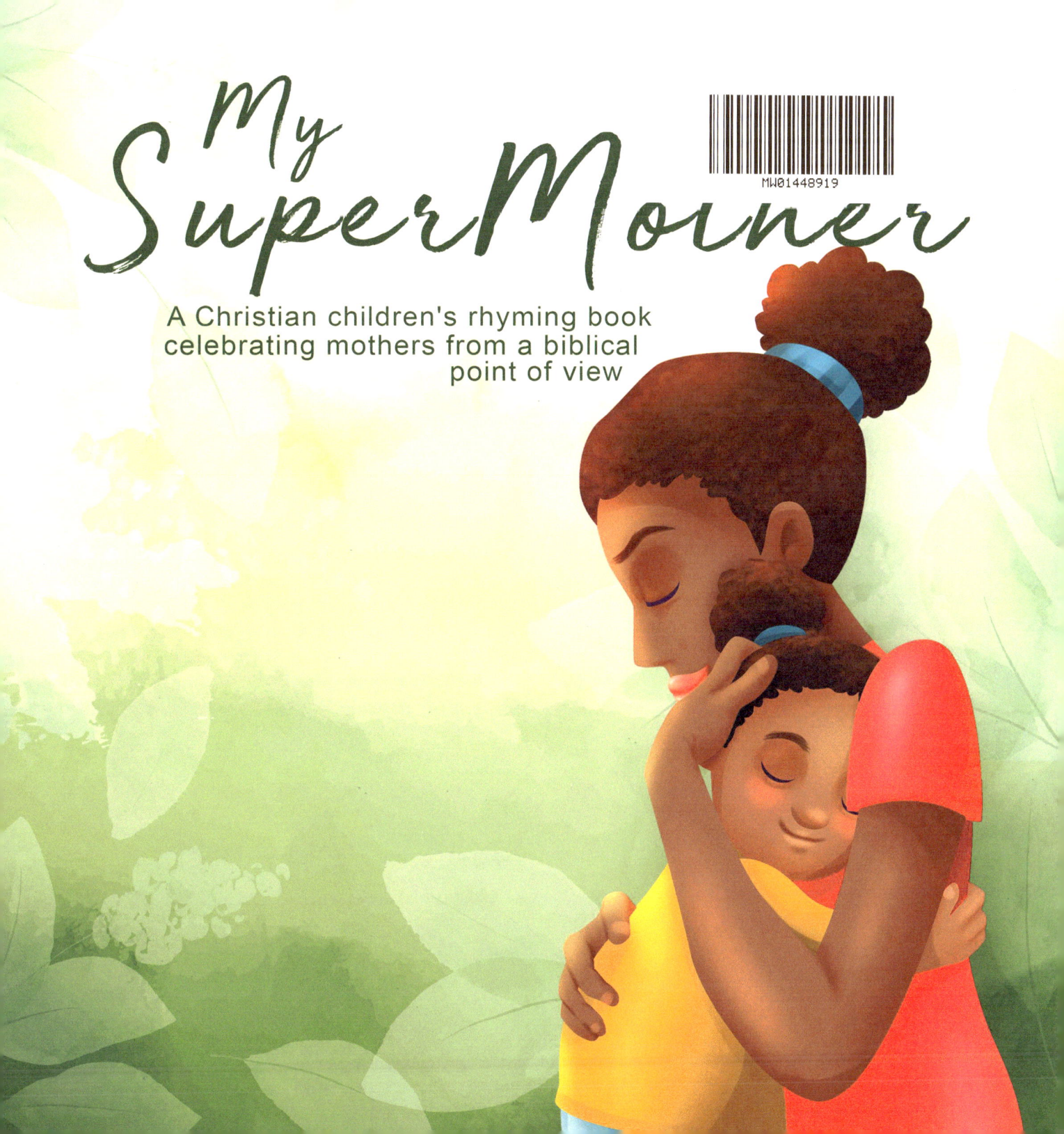

A Christian children's rhyming book celebrating mothers from a biblical point of view

My SuperMother

Coloring Book Edition

A Christian children's rhyming book celebrating mothers from a biblical point of view

Good News Meditations
G.L. Charles

To receive print-ready samples from the coloring book version of this book, please go to gnmkids.com/free

Copyrights

Copyright 2022 by Good News Meditations Kids - All rights reserved

This book or parts thereof may not be reproduced in any form, stored in any retrieval system, or transmitted in any form by any means—electronic, mechanical, photocopy, recording, or otherwise—without prior written permission of the copyright holder.

www.gnmkids.com

This book belongs to:

....

....

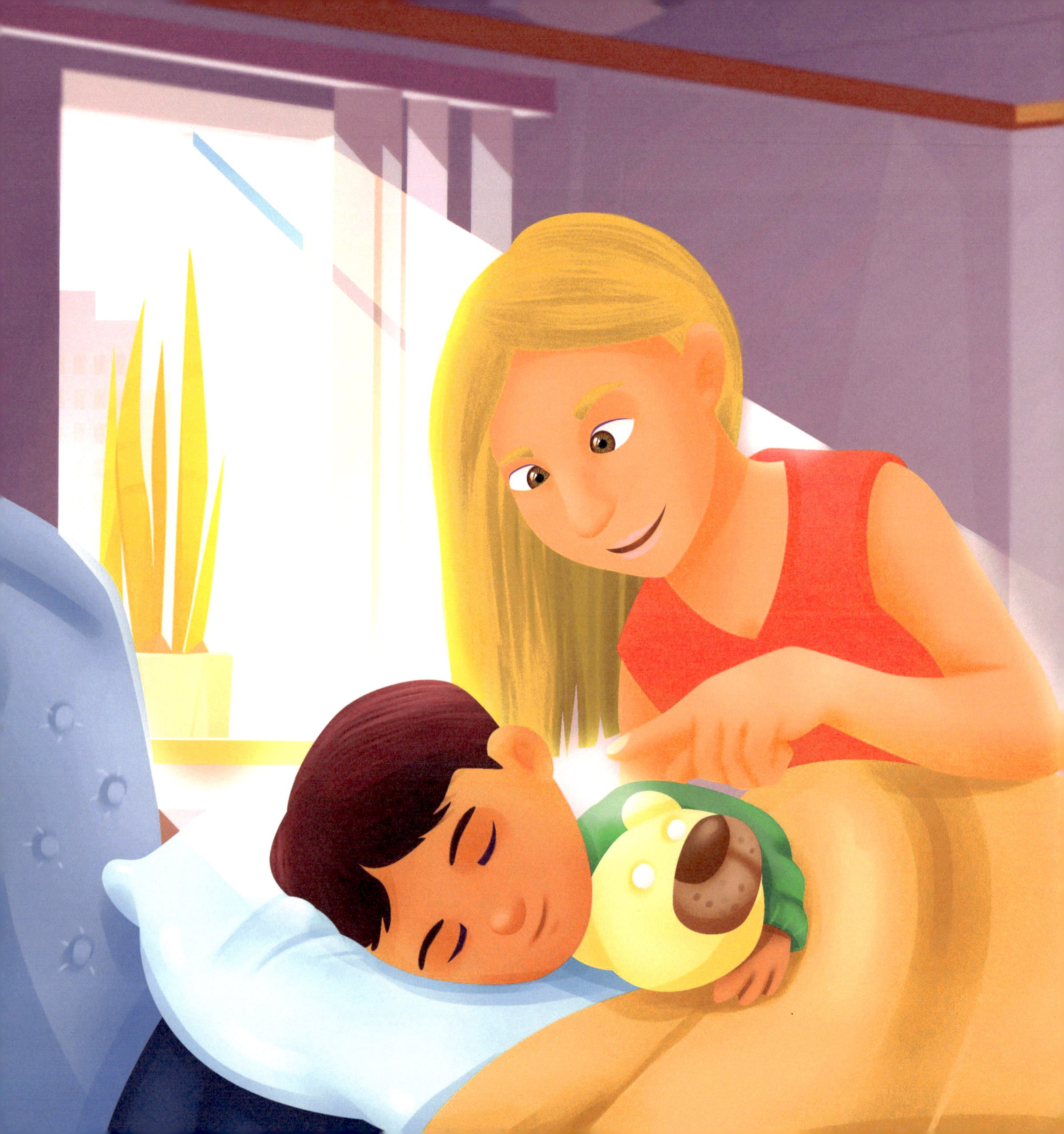

I wake in the morning and what do I see?
My mother's face! She's smiling at me!
She loves and adores me – This I know
For the gleam in her eyes, it tells me so.

My mother's a gift from the Lord up above.
She fills up my heart with her unending love.
She guides and protects me as mothers should do, And delights that I am God's gift to her, too!

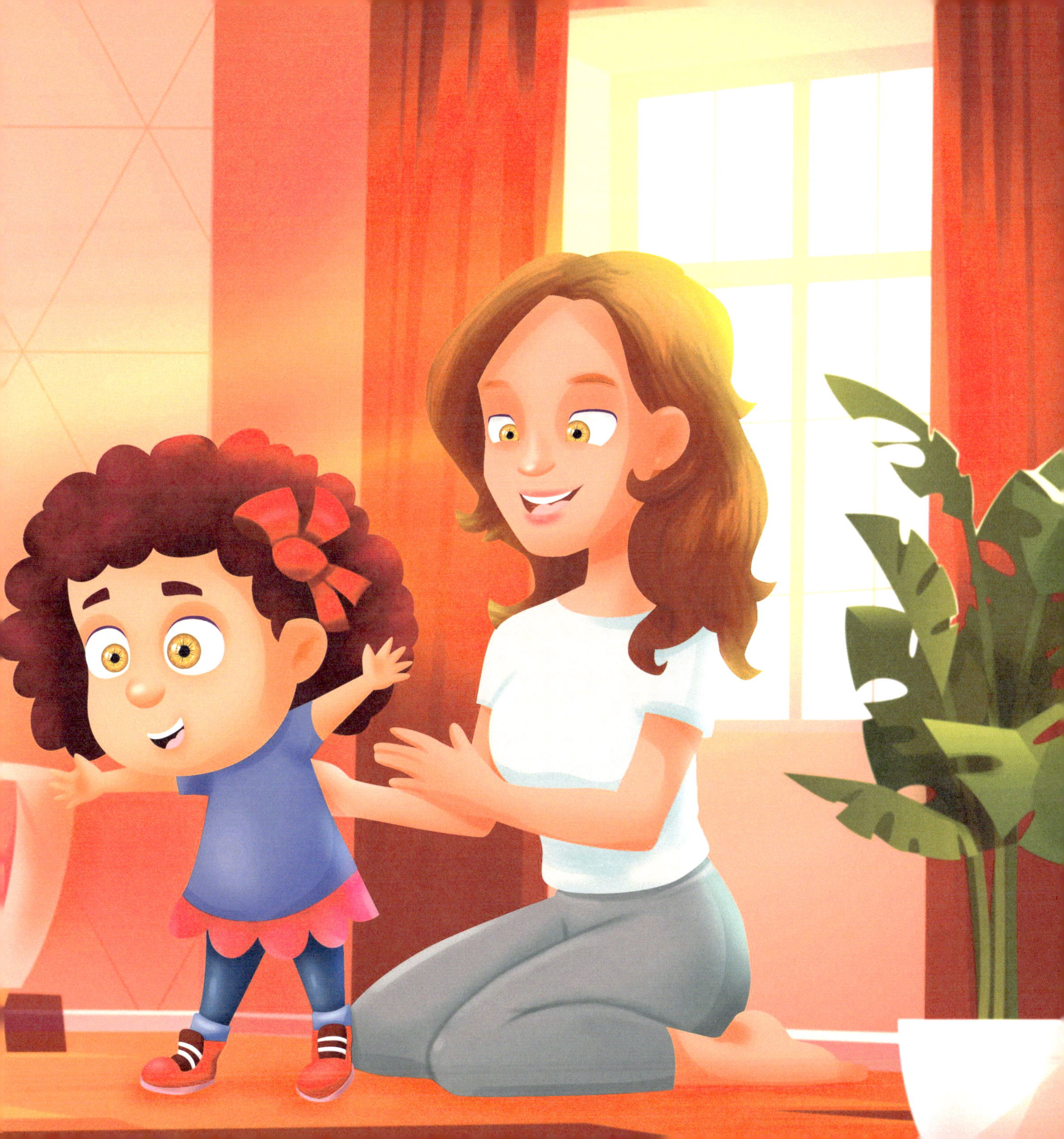

She reads me the Bible, for that's how God shows us
Examples like Jochebed, mother of Moses.
His life was in danger, but she had a plan –
So he lived and grew up to become a great man!

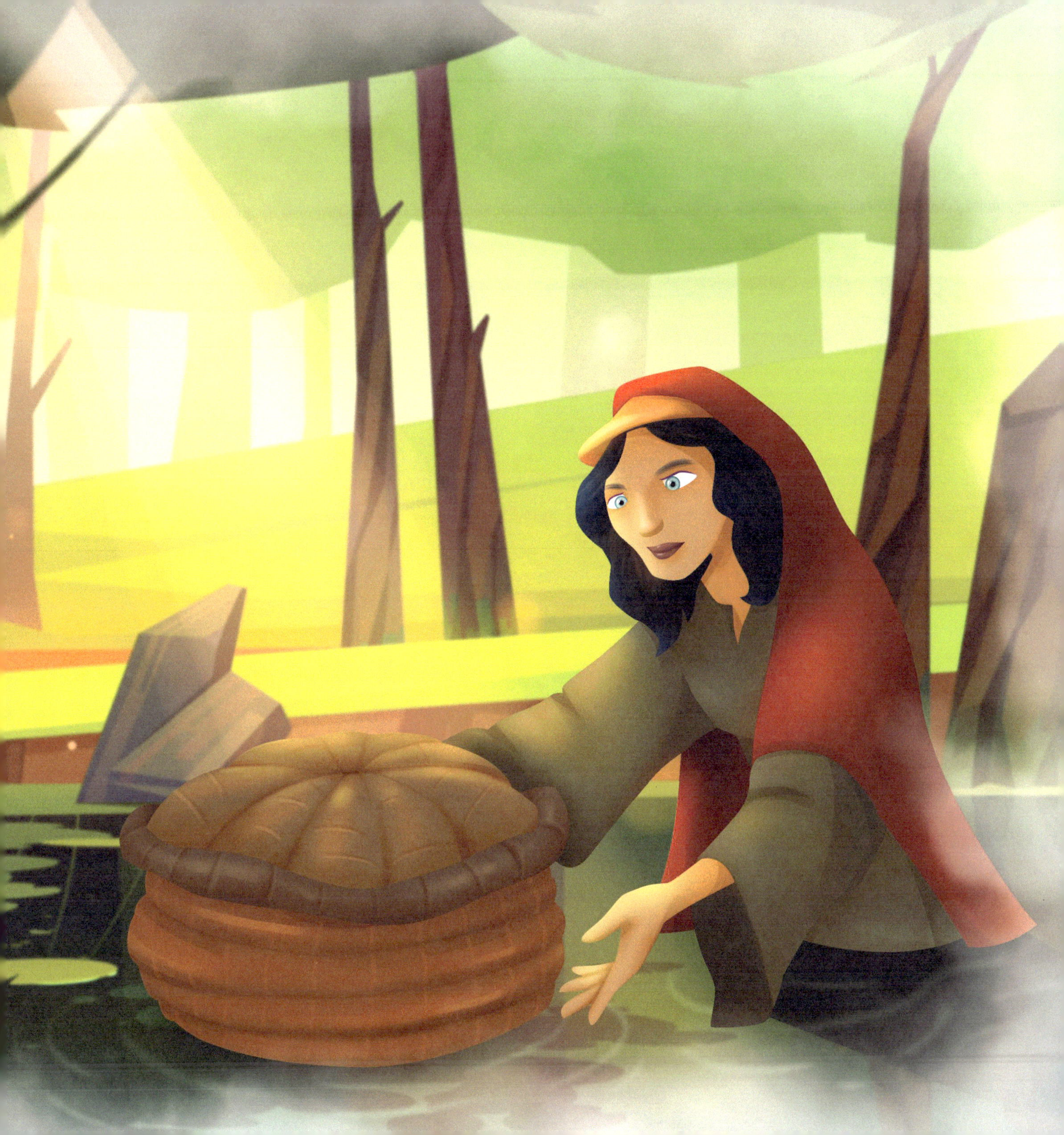

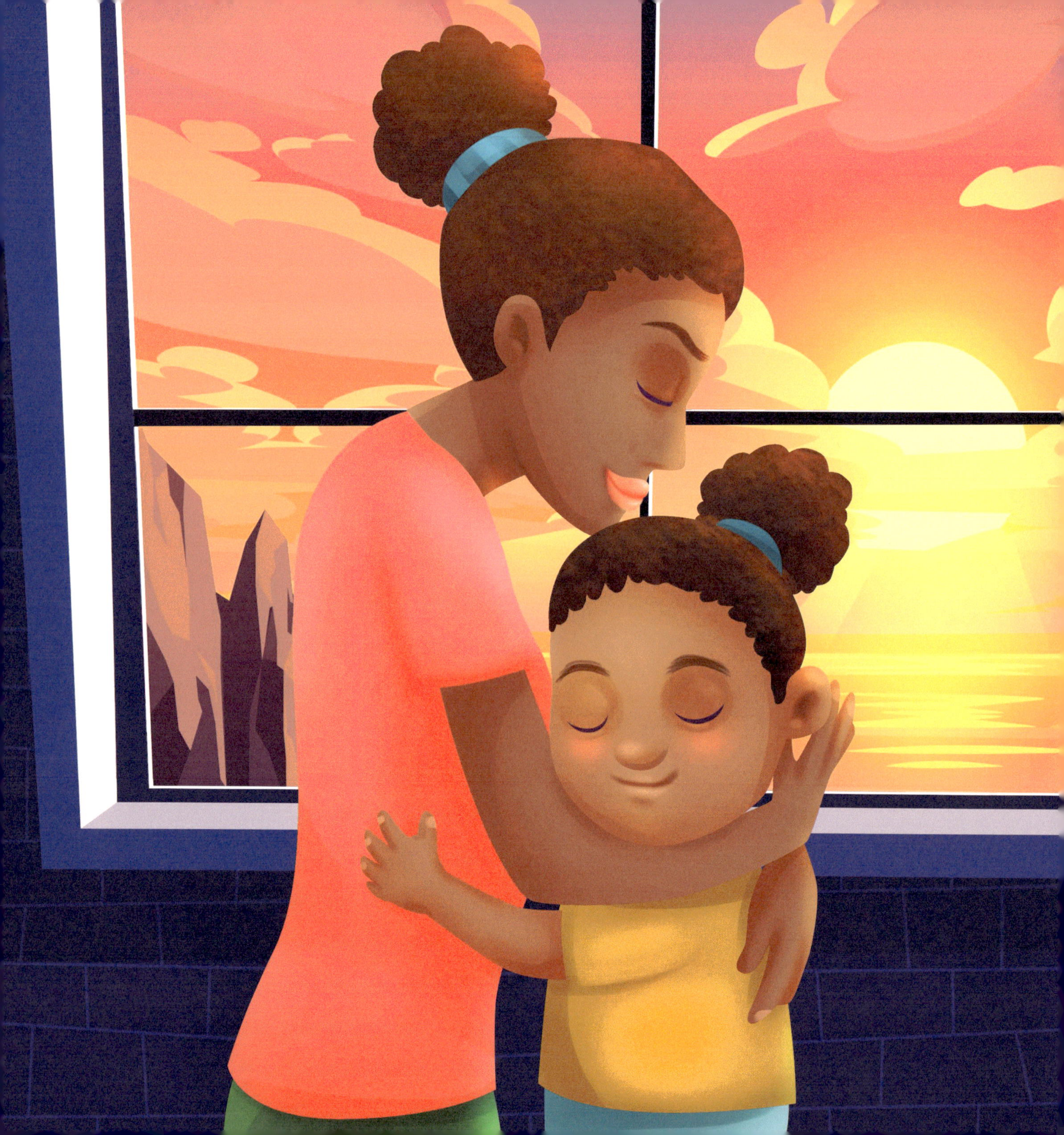

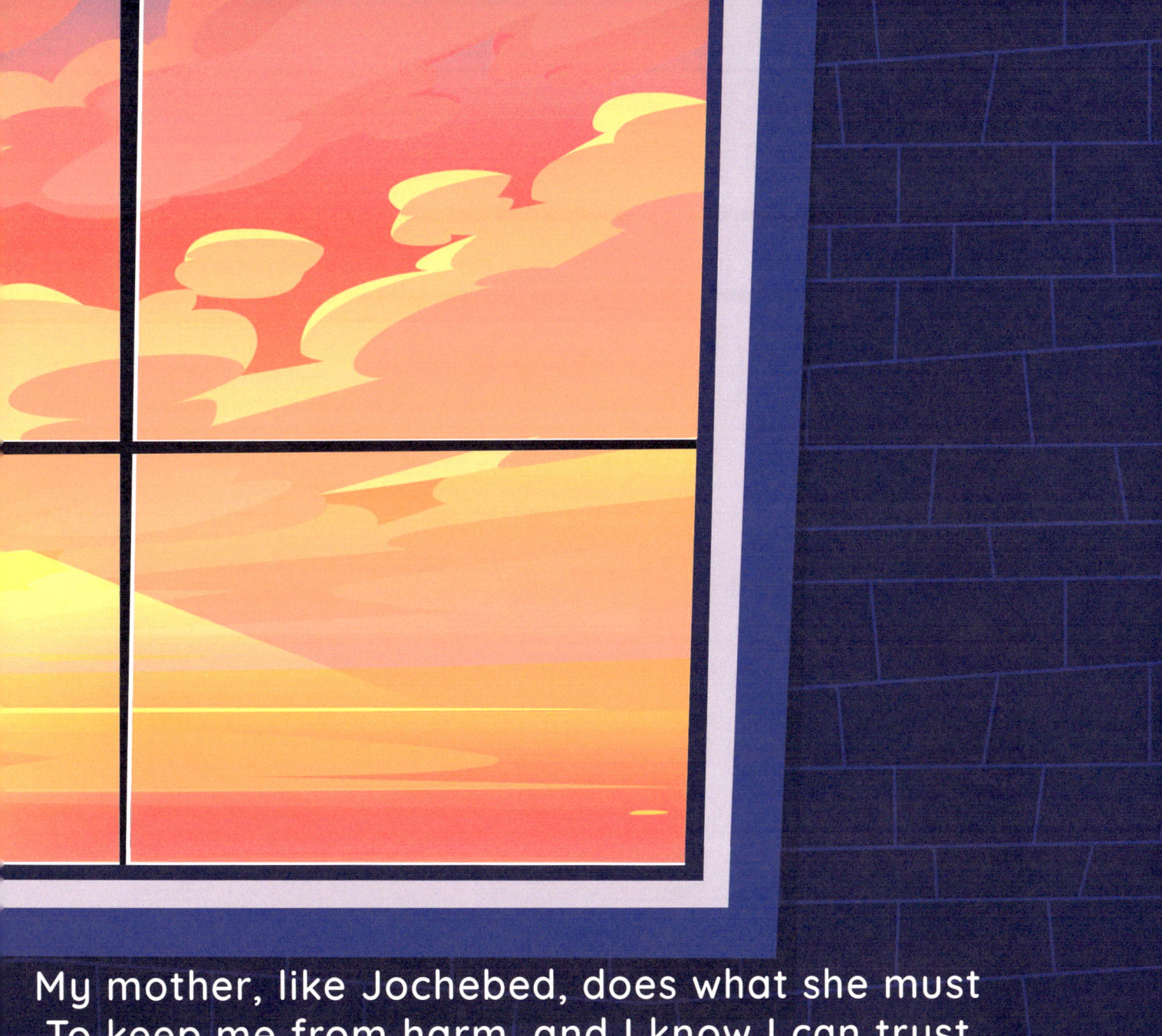

My mother, like Jochebed, does what she must
To keep me from harm, and I know I can trust
Her to do what is best, for by night and by day,
She watches for danger to chase it away.

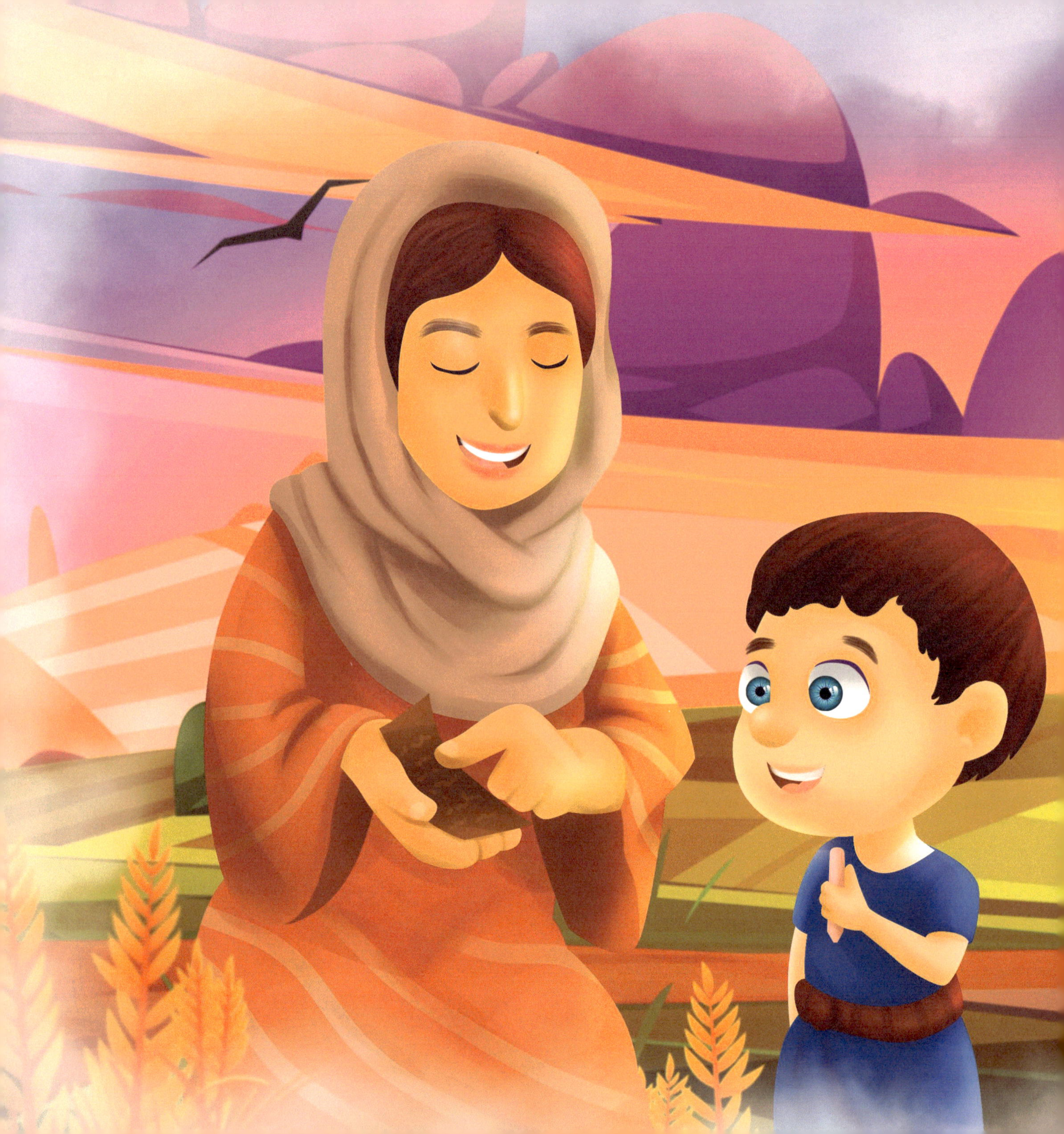

In the Bible we read of Eunice who taught
Her little son, Timothy, things that he ought
To know from the Bible like God's Holy Will –
And when he was grown, he loved the Lord, still!

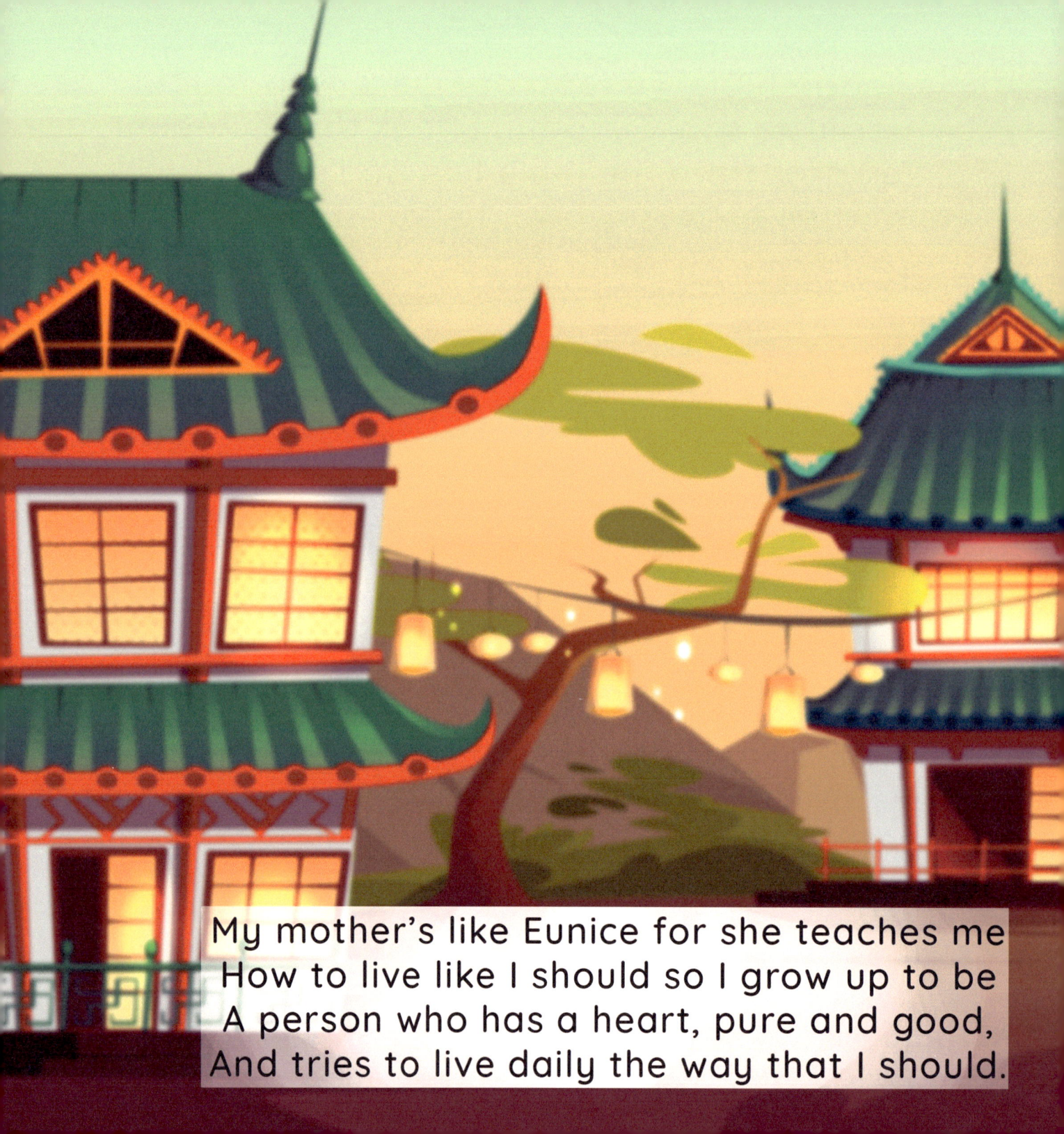

My mother's like Eunice for she teaches me
How to live like I should so I grow up to be
A person who has a heart, pure and good,
And tries to live daily the way that I should.

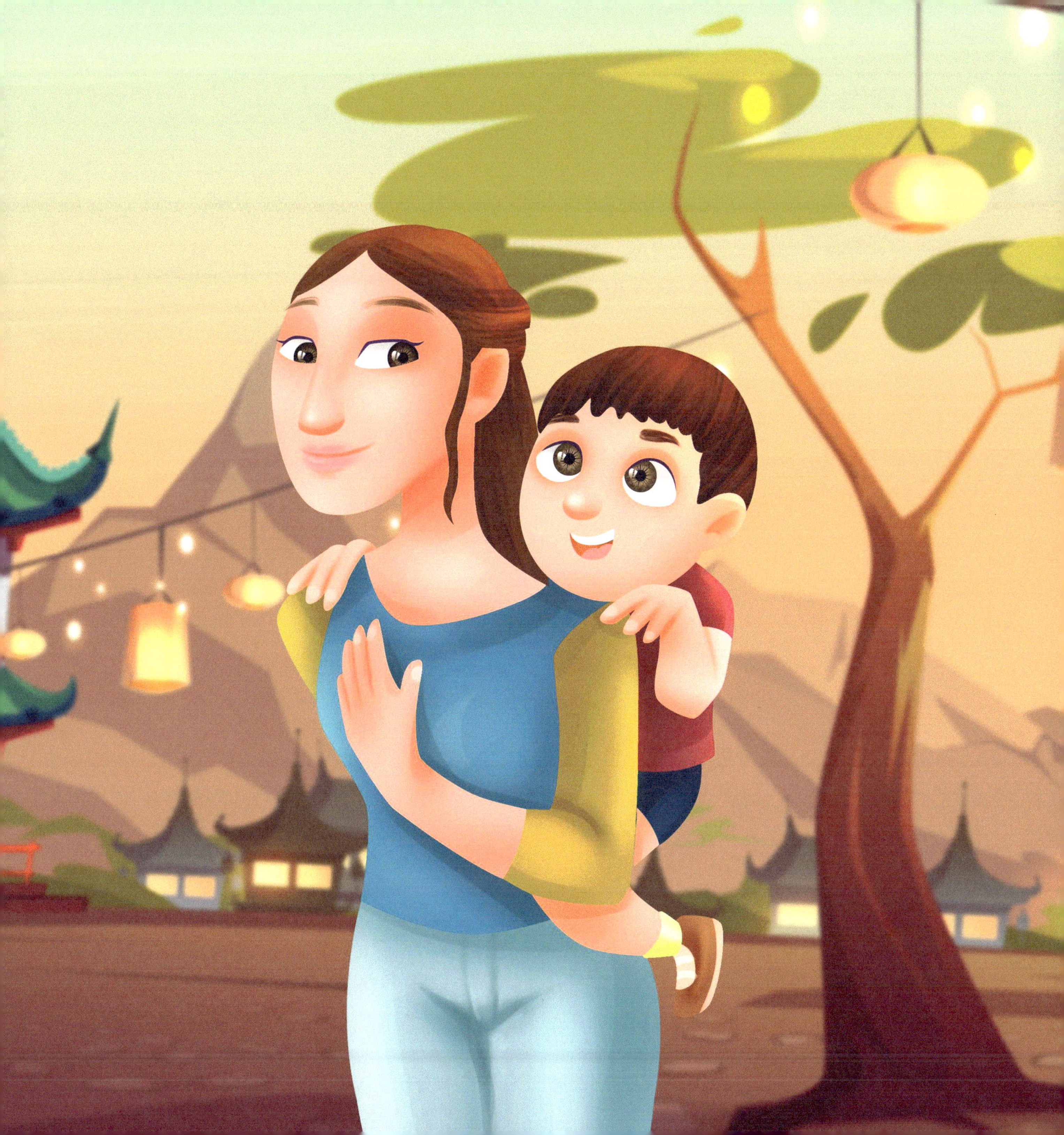

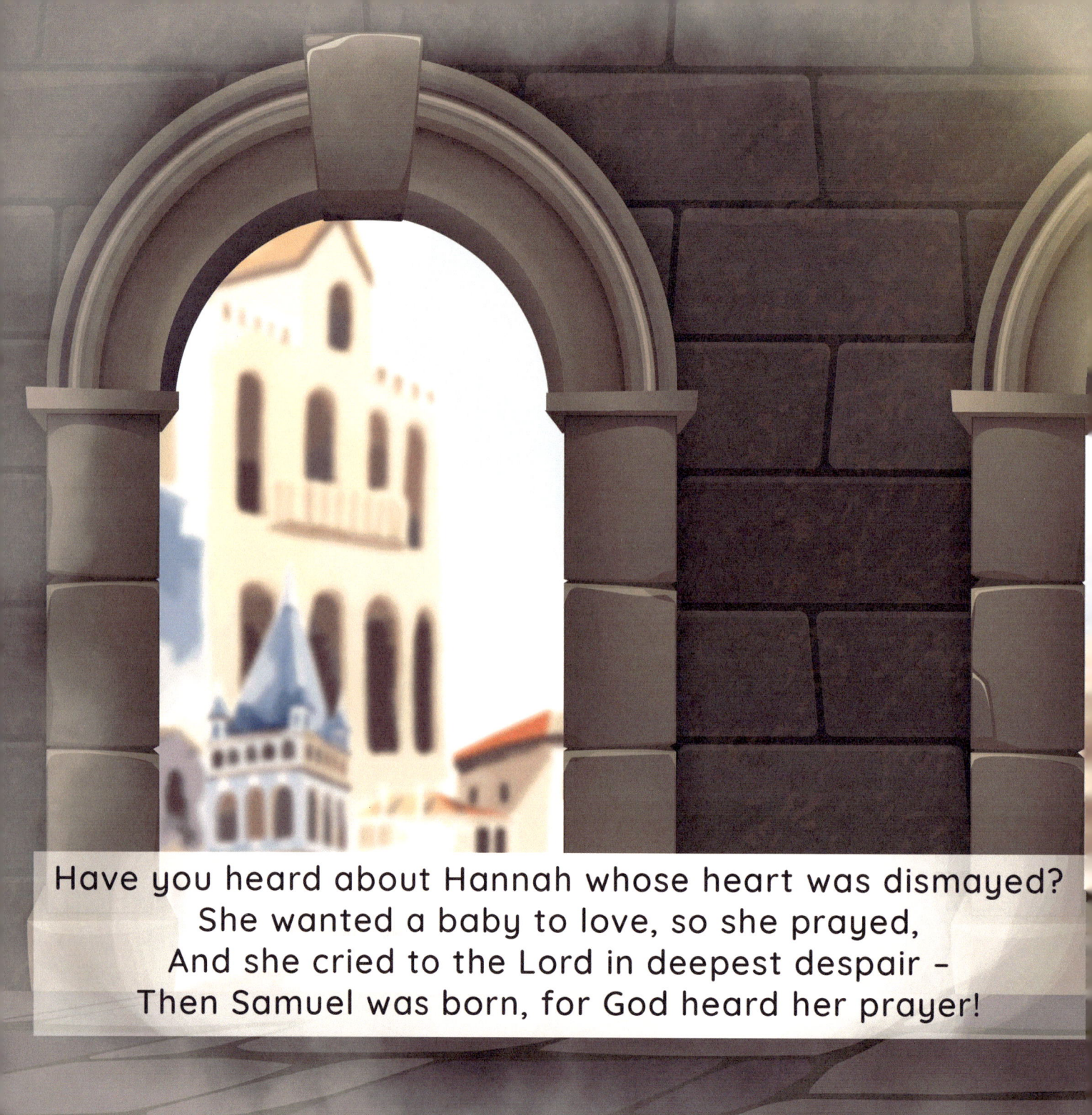

Have you heard about Hannah whose heart was dismayed?
She wanted a baby to love, so she prayed,
And she cried to the Lord in deepest despair –
Then Samuel was born, for God heard her prayer!

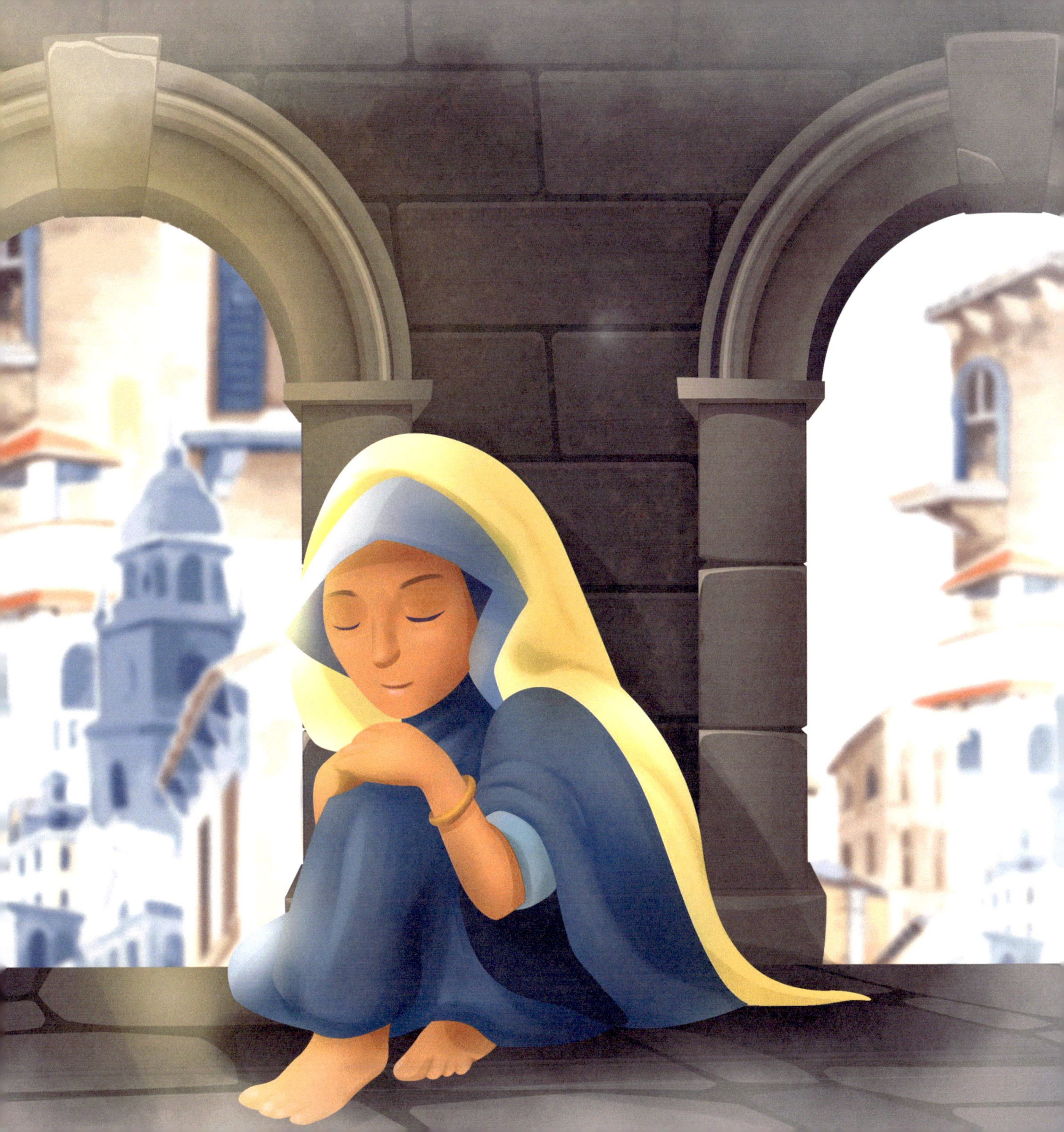

My mother's like Hannah – She prays every day –
Mostly for me that I live the Lord's Way,
Making good choices in all that I do –
(And, like Hannah, I'm sure that she cries for me, too!)

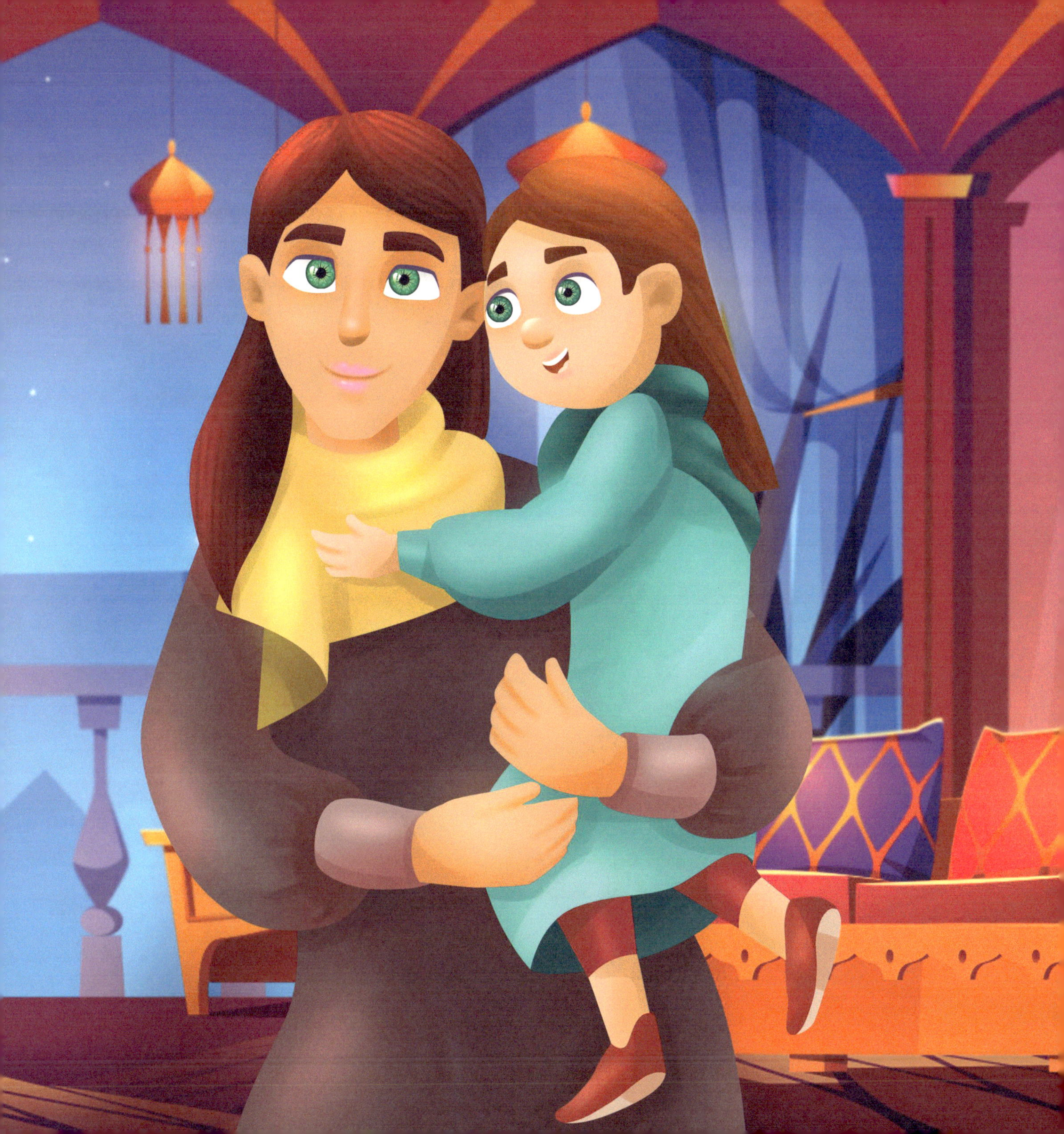

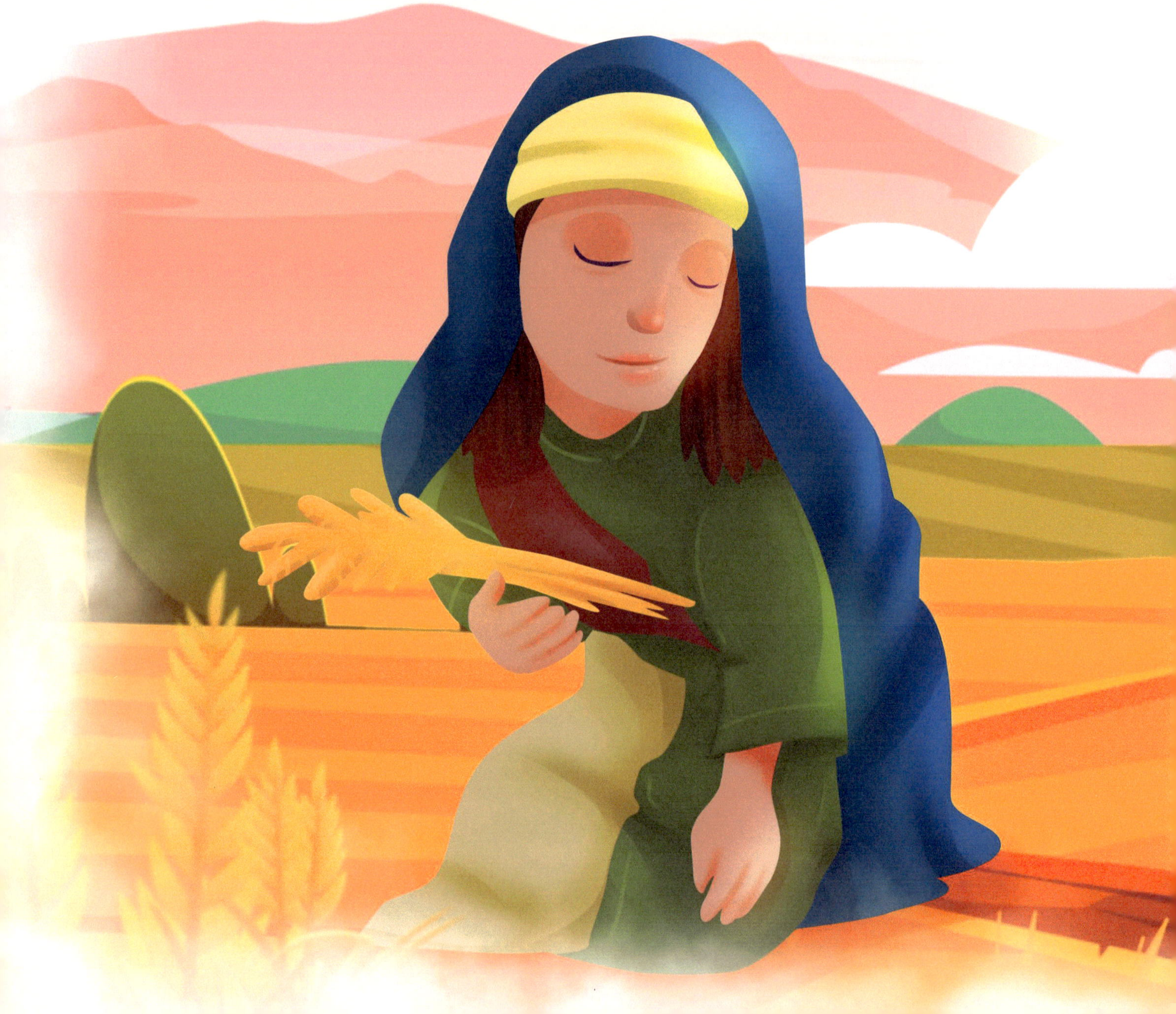

My mother's like Ruth – Though a Gentile from birth,
God showed her grace to prove all people's worth,
And prepare for the coming of Christ, Whose salvation
Reaches all people and includes every nation.

Mary was mother of God's only Son –
An angel said, "Mary, you are the one
Whom God has chosen for this Holy task."
Mary replied, "Lord, I'll do as You ask."

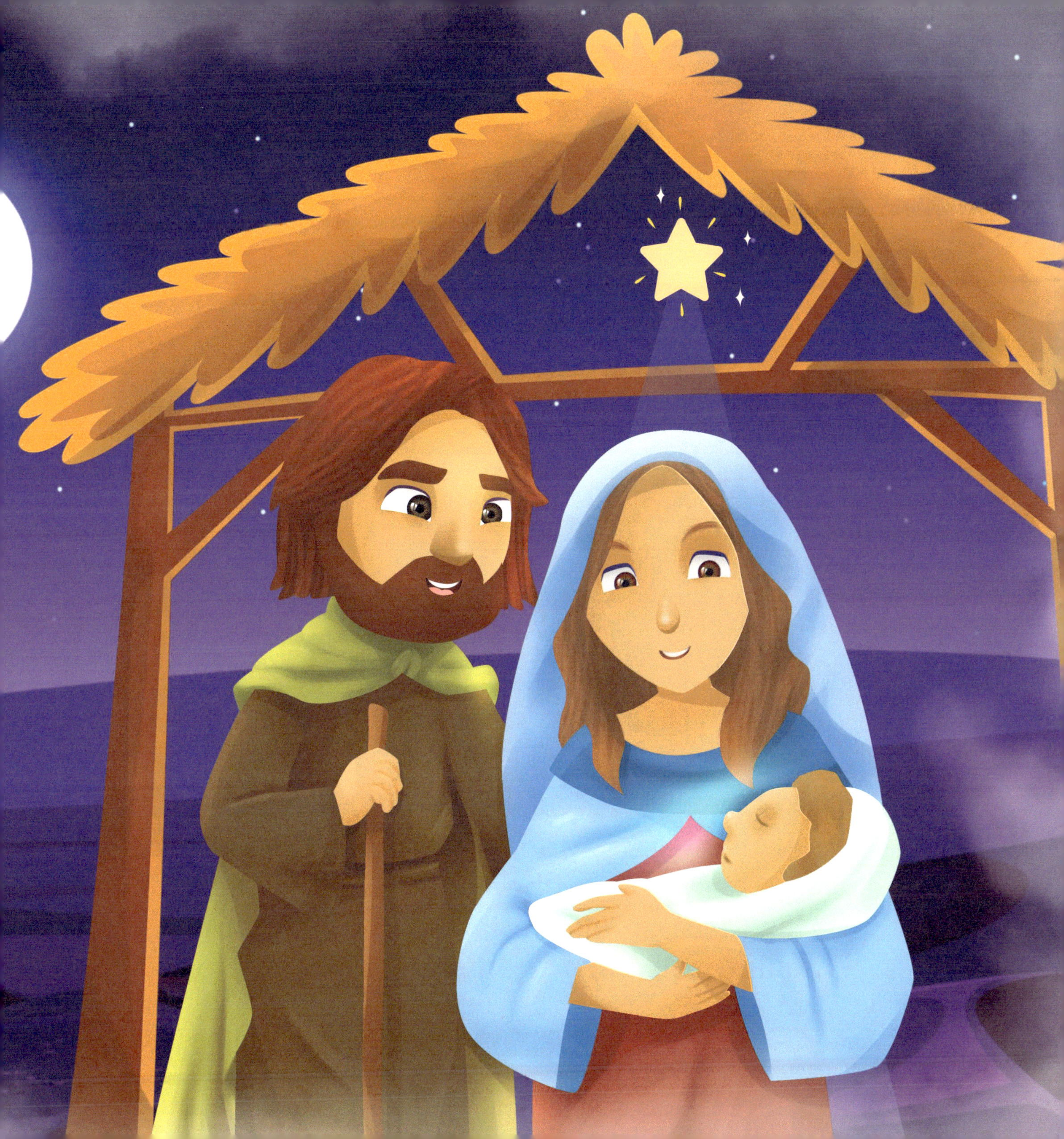

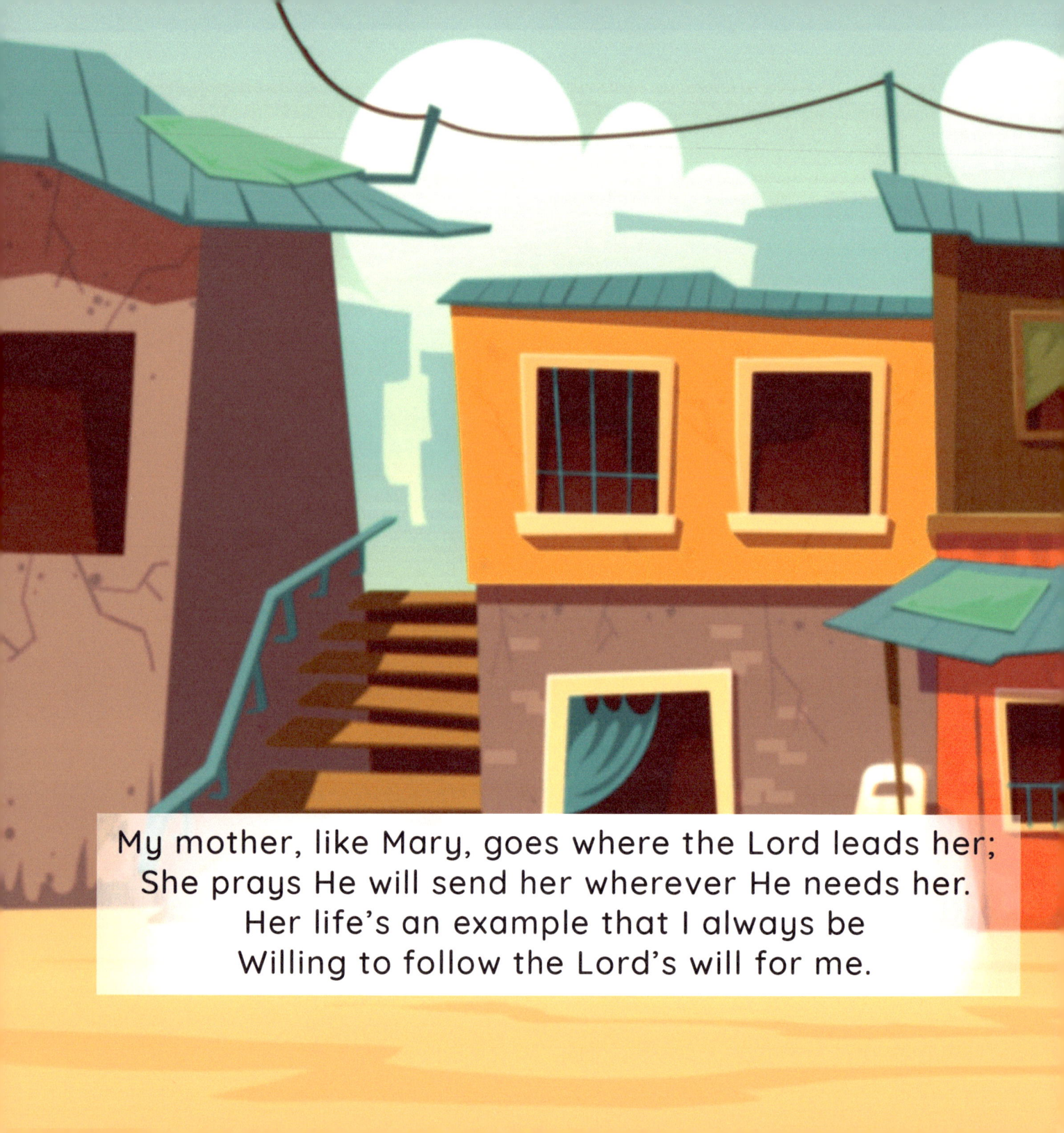

My mother, like Mary, goes where the Lord leads her;
She prays He will send her wherever He needs her.
Her life's an example that I always be
Willing to follow the Lord's will for me.

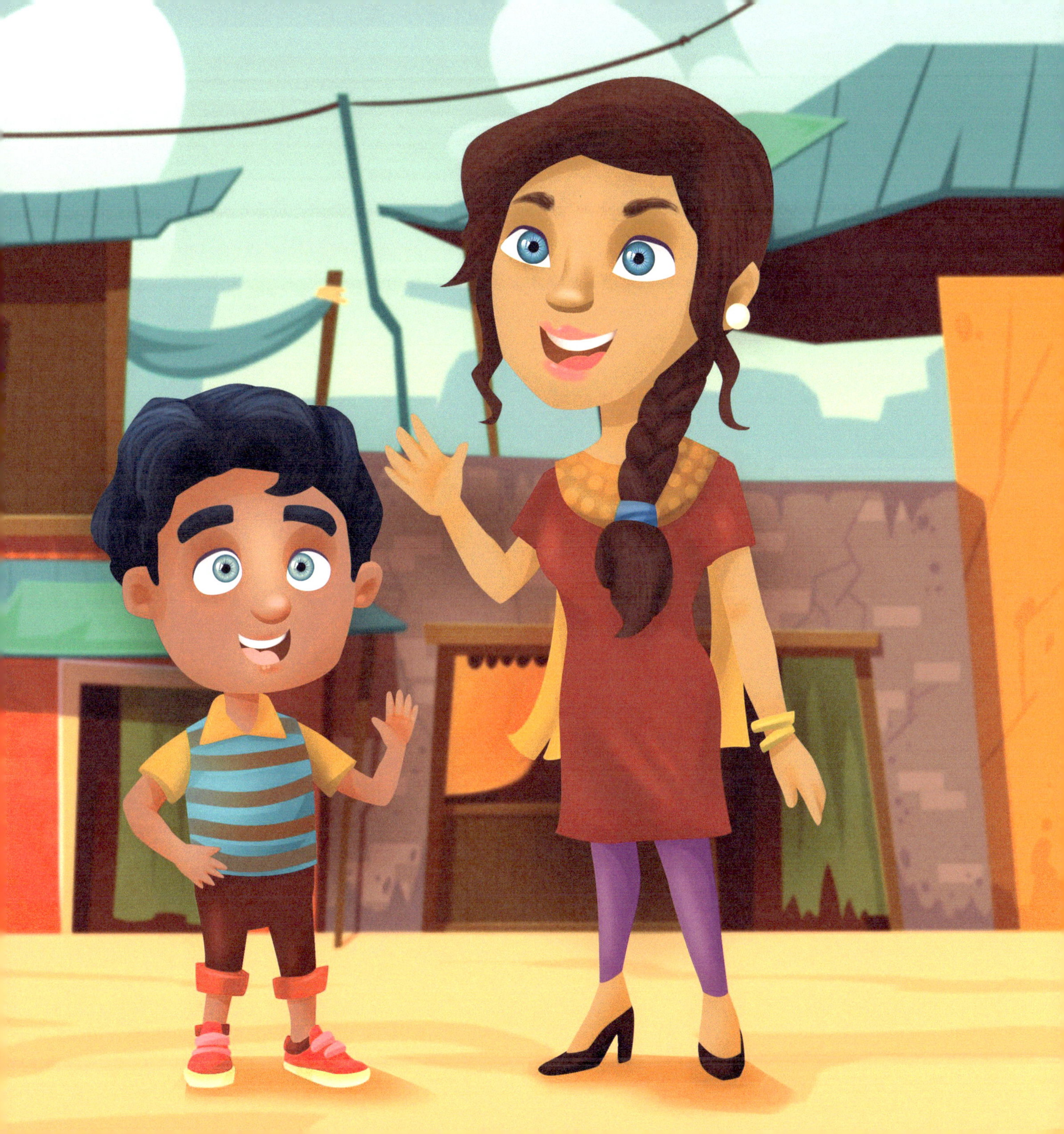

Like the virtuous woman, she's up before dawn,
Making sure that I have clean clothes to put on,
A warm coat in winter, and shoes for my feet.
She keeps our home neat, cooks the meals that we eat.

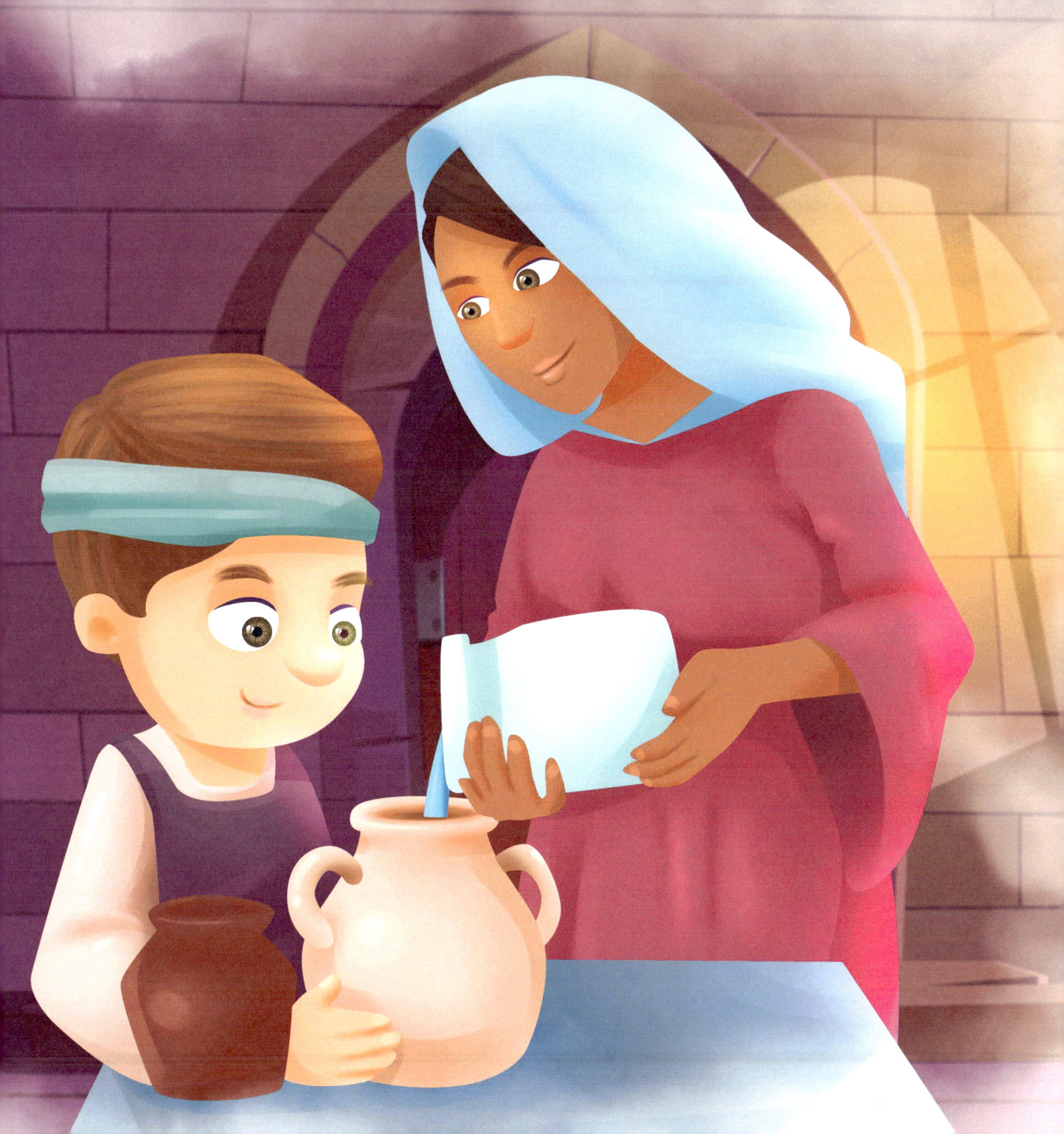

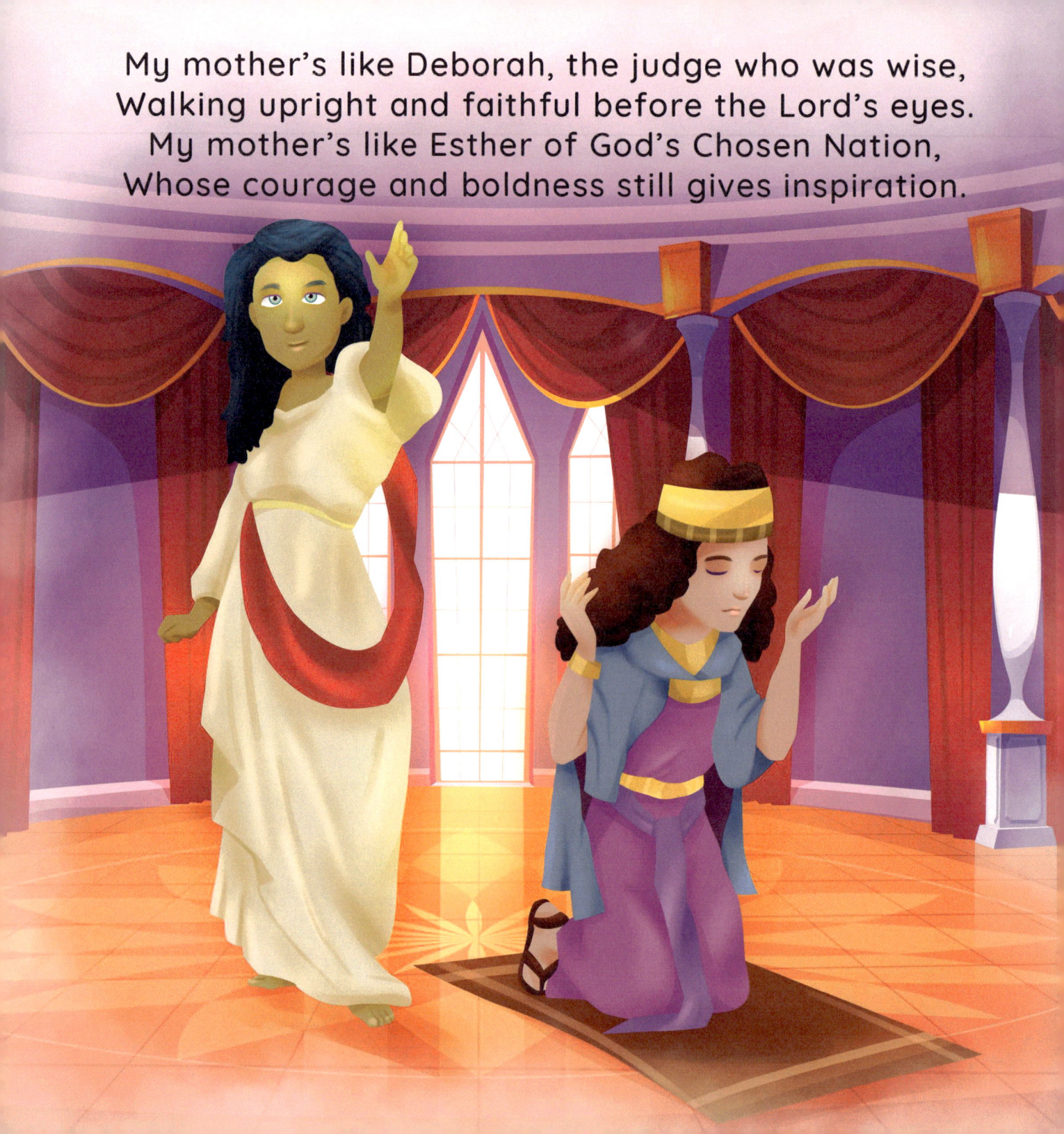

My mother's like Deborah, the judge who was wise,
Walking upright and faithful before the Lord's eyes.
My mother's like Esther of God's Chosen Nation,
Whose courage and boldness still gives inspiration.

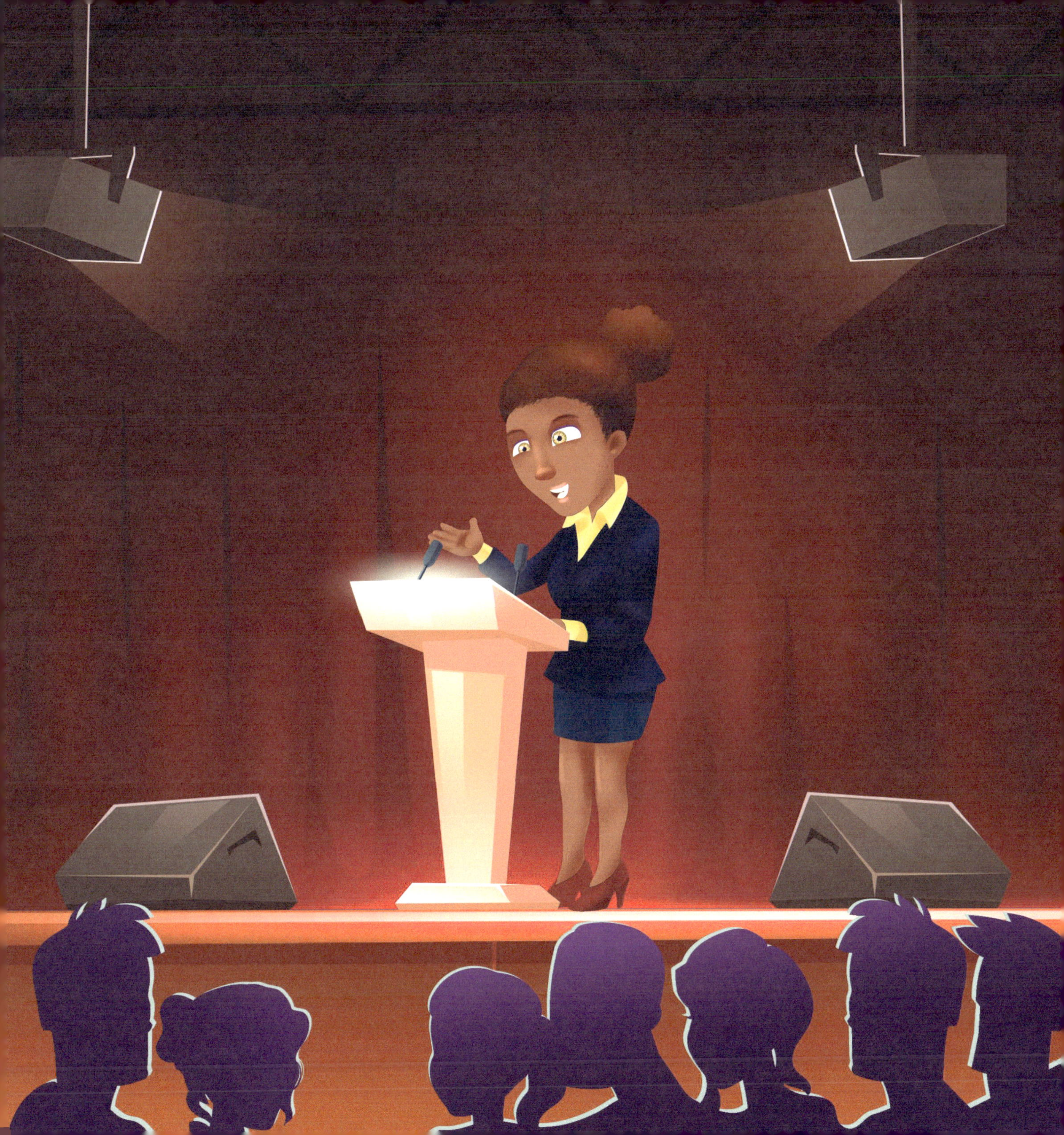

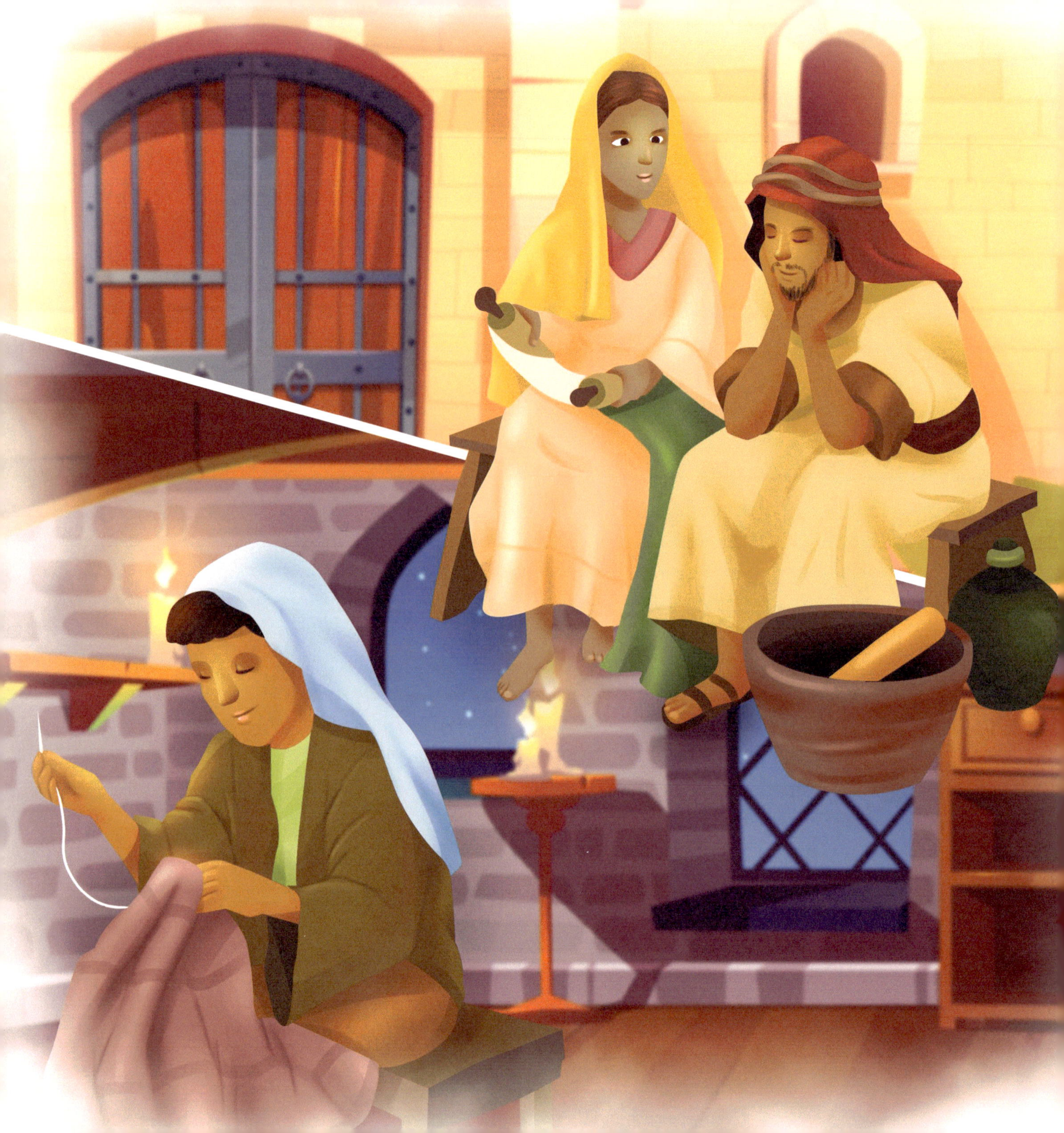

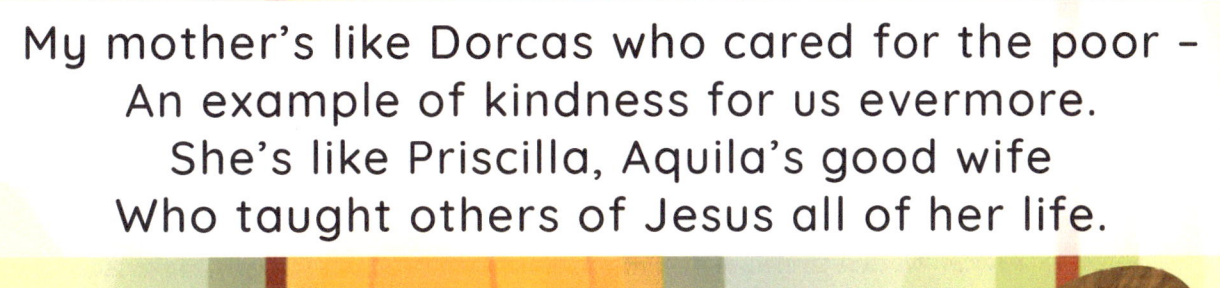

My mother's like Dorcas who cared for the poor –
An example of kindness for us evermore.
She's like Priscilla, Aquila's good wife
Who taught others of Jesus all of her life.

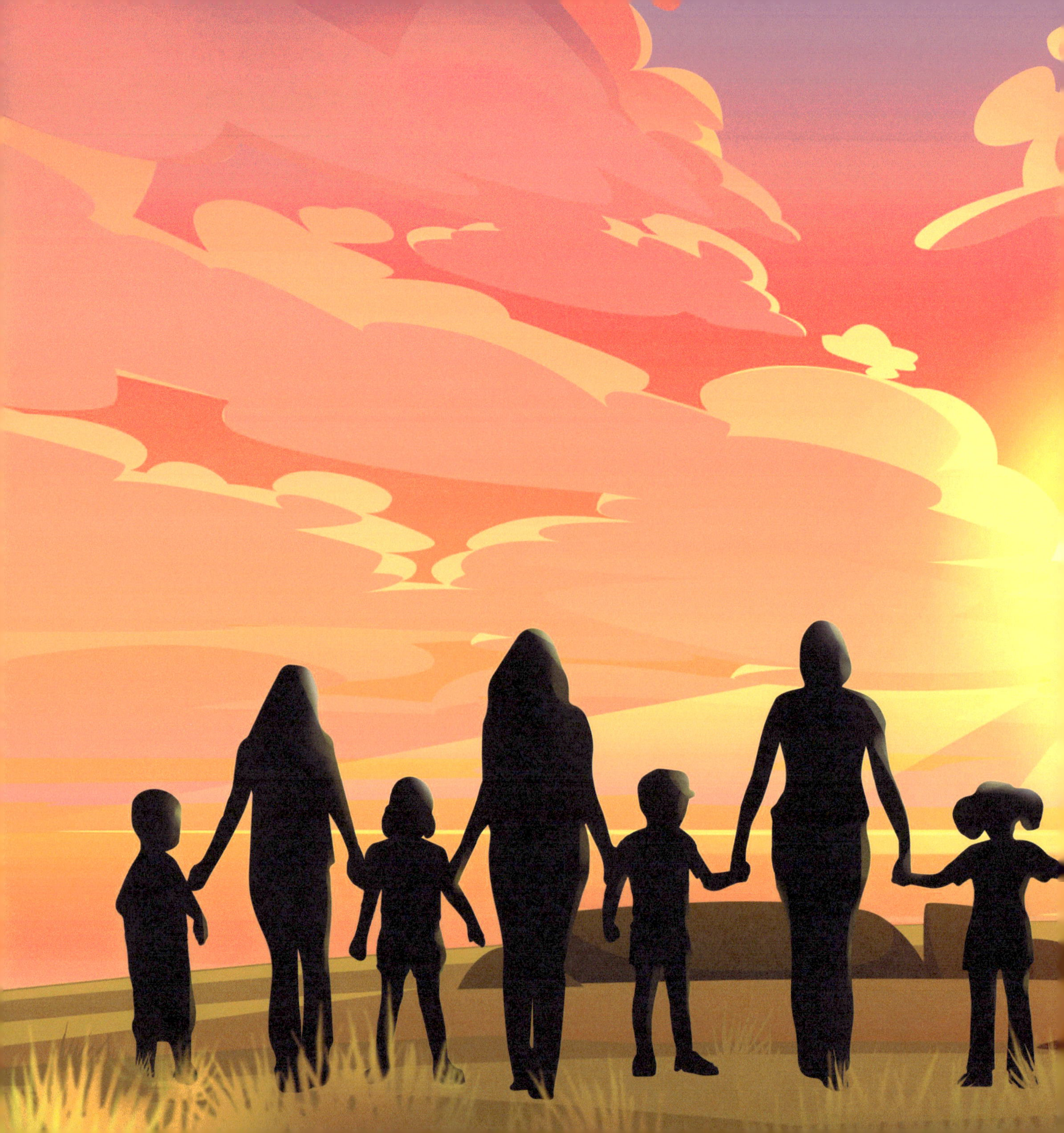

So many women, lived Godly and true –
Just like my mother who loves the Lord, too!
The Lord gave her to me to help me to know
The Lord's love and teachings as daily I grow.

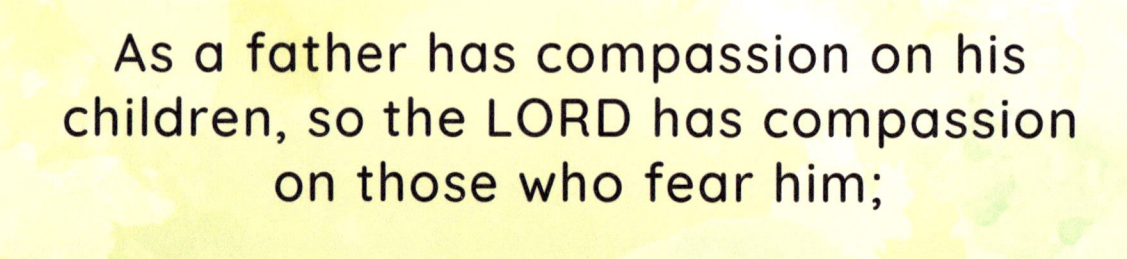

As a father has compassion on his children, so the LORD has compassion on those who fear him;

Psalm 103v13 NIV

Author's note:

Thank you so much for reading this book. If you enjoyed this book, we would love it if you could leave a review and recommend it to a friend.

If there is anything you would like to share with us to help us improve this book, please go to gnmkids.com/feedback

My SuperMother

Coloring Book Edition

A Christian children's rhyming book celebrating mothers from a biblical point of view

Good News Meditations
G.L. Charles

To receive print-ready samples from the coloring book version of this book, please go to gnmkids.com/free

Please checkout our other books

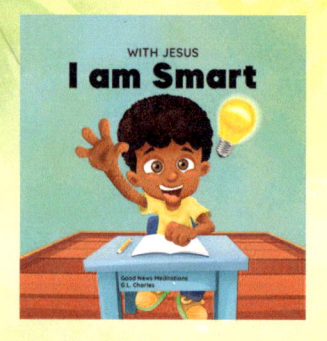

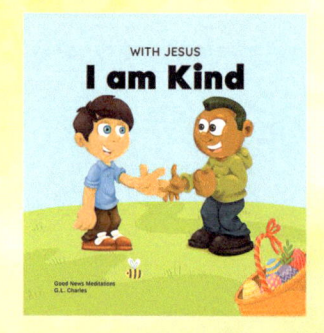

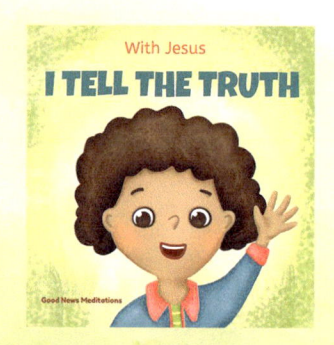

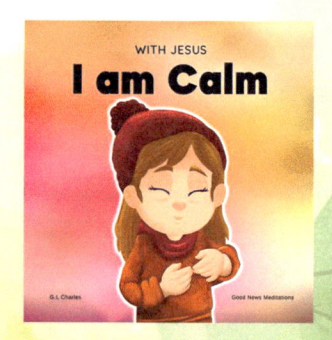

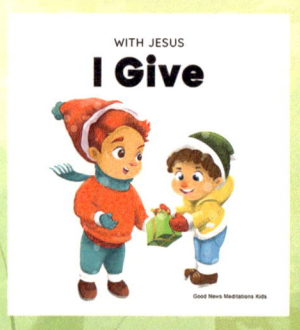

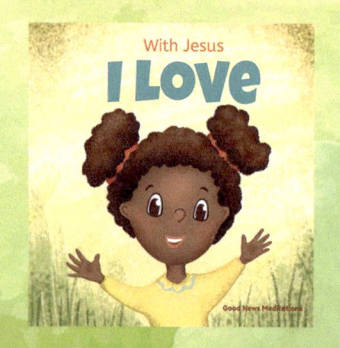

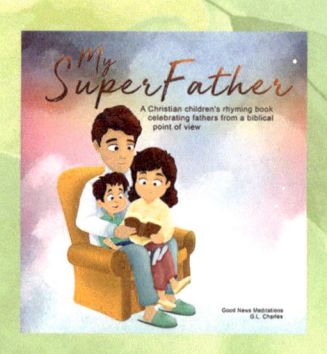

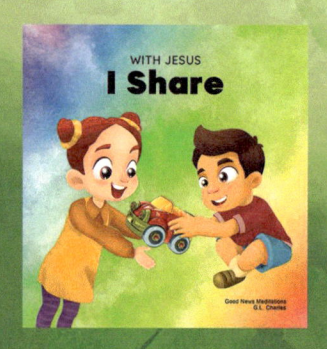

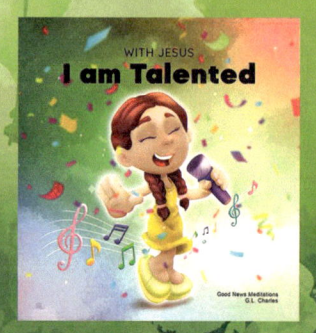

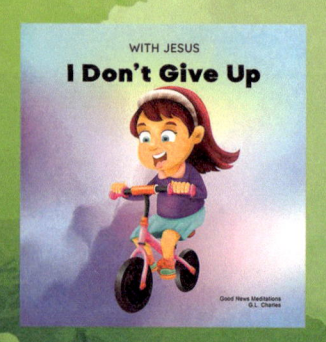

- WITH JESUS — I am Smart
- WITH JESUS — I am Kind
- With Jesus — I TELL THE TRUTH
- WITH JESUS — I am Calm
- WITH JESUS — I am Brave
- WITH JESUS — I Give
- With Jesus — I Love
- My SuperFather — A Christian children's rhyming book celebrating fathers from a biblical point of view
- WITH JESUS — I Share
- WITH JESUS — I am Talented
- WITH JESUS — I Don't Give Up
- With Jesus — I AM THANKFUL

www.gnmkids.com

Made in United States
Troutdale, OR
12/06/2024